For Emilia Rose Williams, and the world around her - B.L.
Pour Léo et Maéva, J'espère que vous visiterez tous ces endroits colorés un jour - A.S.

Quarto is the authority on a wide range of topics.

Quarto educates, entertains and enriches the lives of our readers—enthusiasts and lovers of hands-on living.

www.quartoknows.com

Ben Lerwill has asserted his right to be identified as the author of this work.
Alette Straathof has asserted her right to be identified as the illustrator of this work.

First Published in 2020 by words & pictures,
an imprint of The Quarto Group.
26391 Crown Valley Parkway, Suite 220, Mission Viejo, CA 92691, USA
T: +1 949 380 7510
F: +1 949 380 7575
www.quartoknows.com

A CIP record for this book is available from the Library of Congress.

ISBN: 978 0 7112 4983 7

9 8 7 6 5 4 3 2
Manufactured in Guangdong, China TT052020

MIX
Paper from
responsible sources
FSC® C016973

ONE WORLD MANY COLORS

Ben Lerwill
Alette Straathof

words & pictures

We share one world.
We share many colors.

WHITE shines and sparkles.

It's in the desert of Oman.
An Arabian oryx is moving through the sand dunes.
The animal has strong legs and long sharp horns.

It's in icy Antarctica.

At the bottom of the world, penguins are
swimming and seals are resting on the shore.
The frozen land furls out forever.

It's in sunny Australia.

The Sydney Opera House is moon-bright in the morning light.

Ferries are crossing the harbor and clouds are floating in the sky.

PINK blooms and brightens.

It's in the blossom of Japan.
In springtime, the cherry trees grow thousands
of little flowers. The petals are light and soft.

It's in a sweet-smelling Paris bakery.
Look! Pink macarons and trays full of cakes and pastries. Which treat would you choose?

It's on a wide lake in Kenya.
The flamingos are balancing on long legs.
Some are dipping their beaks in the water.
The birds live under big African skies.

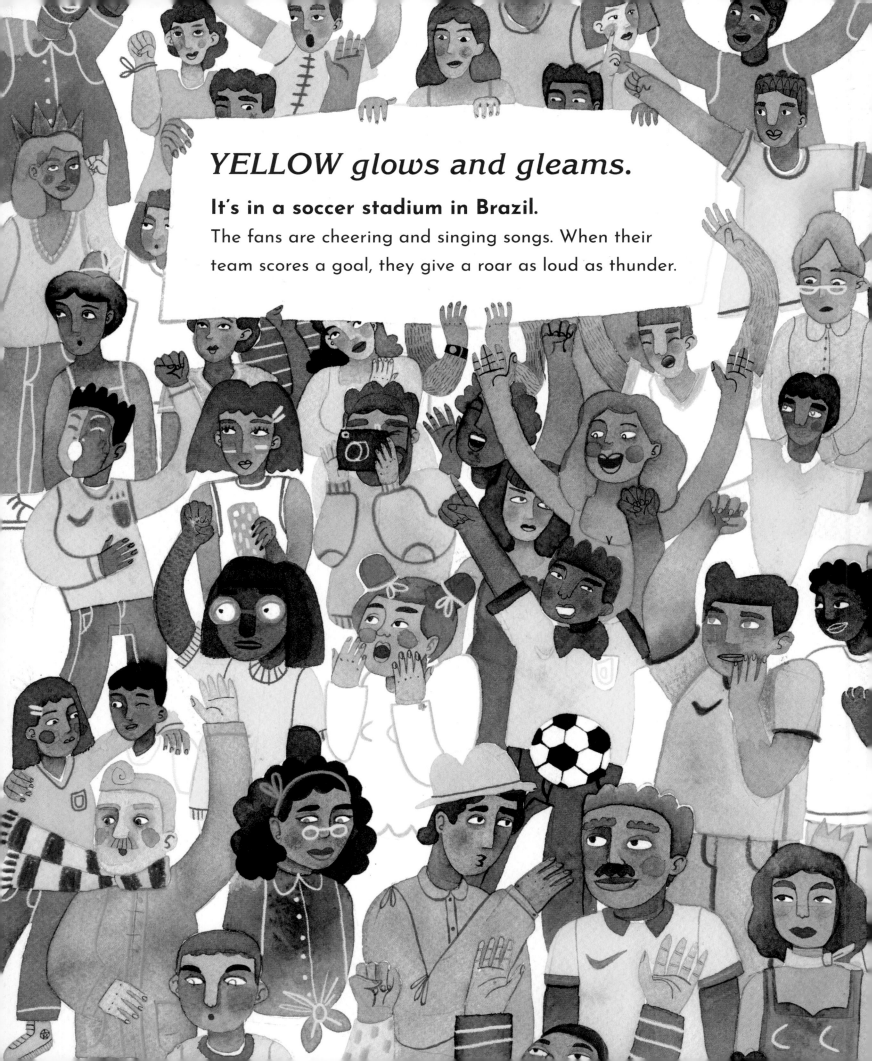

YELLOW glows and gleams.

It's in a soccer stadium in Brazil.

The fans are cheering and singing songs. When their team scores a goal, they give a roar as loud as thunder.

It's on the streets of New York City.
The taxi-cabs are honking their horns.
People are hurrying this way and that,
under buildings that stretch up to the sky.

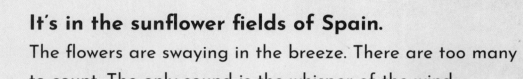

It's in the sunflower fields of Spain.
The flowers are swaying in the breeze. There are too many
to count. The only sound is the whisper of the wind.

BLUE shimmers and soars.

It's in the deep ocean.
The blue whale is the giant of the seas, the biggest animal on Planet Earth. Its enormous tail moves slowly and steadily as it swims.

It's in the sky above Mount Everest.
The mountain is so high that it can take two
whole months for climbers to reach the top.

It's in the Canadian woods in winter.
Shh! It's a blue jay. All the trees are
covered in glittering snow. The bird's
bright feathers help to keep it warm.

GREEN glistens and grows.

It's in the wilds of South Africa.
A chameleon is slinking along a branch.
It's green now, but it has a secret—it can
change color to match its background.

It's in the countryside of Vietnam.
The farmers in the rice field are wearing
wide hats to shelter from the sun. The field
is very green, so the rice is nearly ready.

It's in the Amazon Rainforest.
The tangled green jungle is swarming
with life. Monkeys and toucans, jaguars
and parrots, butterflies and snakes.
How many animals can you see?

RED dances and dreams.

It's in Hong Kong at Chinese New Year.
Lanterns are hanging in rows and
fireworks are bursting in the night sky.
The lanterns give off a rosy glow.

It's in London at rush hour.
A double-decker bus is driving across Westminster Bridge.
Drifting everywhere are the noises of the city.

It's in Egypt at sunset.
The Pyramids are old, mighty, and silent. As the day ends,
the sun's last rays wash the ancient stones in red light.

We share one world.

We share many colors.

The world we share

Our journey around the world has taken us from busy cities to wild jungles, showing us some of the special colors that we share. Can you spot all the different things we've seen?

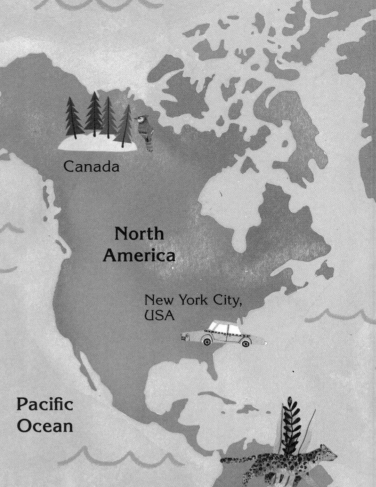

Canada

North America

New York City, USA

Pacific Ocean

Amazon Rainforest

Brazil

South America

White

blanco... weiß... أبيض *... blanc...* 白色*... λευκό...* 白*... hvit*
An Arabian oryx in the desert
The frozen ice of Antarctica
The Sydney Opera House in Australia

Pink

rosado... rosa... وردي *... rose...* 粉色*... ρόζ...* ピンク*... rosa*
Cherry blossom in Japan
Macarons in a Paris bakery
A flamingo on a Kenyan lake

Yellow

amarillo... gelb... أصفر *... jaune...* 黄色*... κίτρινος...* 黄色*... gul*
A football shirt in Brazil
A taxi cab in New York City
A sunflower in Spain

Blue

azul... blau... أزرق *... bleu...* 藍色*... μπλέ...* 青*... blå*
A blue whale in the ocean
The sky above Mount Everest
A blue jay in a Canadian forest

Arctic
Ocean

London,
UK

Europe

Asia

Paris,
France

Mount Everest

Spain

Japan

Egypt

Africa

Hong Kong, China

Kenya

Arabian
Desert

Vietnam

Atlantic
Ocean

Indian
Ocean

Sydney,
Australia

South Africa

Oceania

Green

verde... grün... أخضر... vert... 綠色... πράσινος... 緑... grønn

A chameleon in South Africa
Rice fields in Vietnam
The Amazon Rainforest

Southern
Ocean

Red

rojo... rot... أحمر... rouge... 紅色... TO KÓKKIVO... 赤... rød

A temple in Hong Kong
A London bus
The pyramids in Egypt

Antarctica

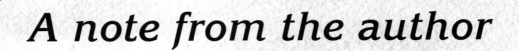

A note from the author

Have you ever seen a rainbow? A really strong, bright rainbow? I think it's one of the most amazing sights in the world. All those popsicle colors, striped across the sky in a perfect curve. Red, orange, yellow, green, blue, indigo, and violet. They light up the sky, and then they are gone.

As I'm sure you know, rainbows usually appear when the weather is sunny and rainy at the same time. I like to think this reminds us how varied life can be. Sun and rain. Deserts and oceans. Thick rainforests and noisy markets. But while every single city, forest, and sea is one of a kind, they all have things in common too. The yellow we see in a wildflower is the same yellow we see on a tropical fish. The red of a strawberry is the red of a fire engine. Colors help to make our planet the amazing place that it is.

I live in England, but I've been lucky enough to spend time in places all over the world. If there's one thing this has taught me, it's that everywhere, and everyone, is connected. We might have different languages and beliefs, different foods and traditions, but we all share the same world. That's why it's so important that we cherish it.

Ben

Alette